praise

about *muted*

"This utterly brilliant short work is not merely dystopian; that is too easy a label. It is a wholly organic, poetic warning of a future where a master may 'dress his staff in false expression' and other, more dire, imaginings. There are too many gifted turns of phrase and images for this to not be regarded as an extraordinary outpouring of poetic narrative. The protagonist's voice has been tampered with: Bell's voice speaks for her, and movingly."

CHARLES BANE, POET LAUREATE NOMINEE OF FLORIDA

about *she*

"Just beautiful. I read it several times and each time was more painfully beautiful."

MONICA BHIDE, AUTHOR OF
KARMA AND THE ART OF BUTTER CHICKEN

about the author

Jessica Bell is an Australian award-winning author and poet, writing and publishing coach, and graphic designer who lives in Athens, Greece. In addition to her novels and poetry collections, and her best-selling *Writing in a Nutshell* series, she has published a variety of works online and in literary journals, including *Writer's Digest*.

Jessica is also the Co-Founder and Publisher of *Vine Leaves Press & Literary Journal*, a singer/songwriter/guitarist, a voice-over actor, and a freelance editor and writer for English Language Teaching publishers worldwide such as Macmillan Education and Education First.

Before she started writing she was just a young woman with a "useless" Bachelor of Arts degree and a waitressing job.

Visit Jessica's website: *jessicabellauthor.com*

Muted & She: two short stories in verse
Copyright © 2016 Jessica Bell
All rights reserved.

Vine Leaves Press
Melbourne, Victoria, Australia

Collected Edition
ISBN-13: 978-1-925417-52-4

First editions of each story were published separately by Vine Leaves
Press in Canada and Australia, 2013 and 2014

Cover design by Jessica Bell
Interior design by Amie McCracken

National Library of Australia Cataloguing-in-Publication entry: (pbk)
Creator: Bell, Jessica Carmen, author.
Title: Muted & she : two short stories in verse / Jessica Bell.
Edition: Collected edition.
ISBN: 9781925417524 (paperback)
Subjects: Australian poetry.
Stories in rhyme.
Dewey Number: A821.4

muted
& she

two short stories in verse

jessica bell

Vine Leaves Press
Melbourne, Vic, Australia

for those who like to eat words

contents

muted

Concetta depresses
an aluminium slat
of blind
with her forefinger and
gazes into the street,
numb to the snap
of solitude.

Bare feet pass
by her shoebox window
broken, at eye-level,
thriving on nude routine.

She stifles a yawn
and clicks her tongue
in the rear of her cheek
to deactivate
the alarm chip
embedded
into her cochlea,
illegally programmed
with thirty seconds
of her own voice.

The voice she had
before being sentenced
to a life
of silence

for wearing clothes
and singing
a cappella
in an 'instrumental zone.'

She wasn't
even busking
that day,
but on route to
an interview
to be the Queen's
personal music box.

The Queen
is a man
with five fingers and toes.

Newborns only have four.

She swallows
a build-up
of thyme-flavoured saliva
from the tea she drinks
to soothe her throat

and buckles
in pain.
The immune
assistants strapped her to

a chair, forced
her mouth
open
and slashed
her vocal chords.
Surgically
perforated
her eardrums.

The taste of toxic sweat
still lingers on her gums
even more than the memory
of torturers' penises
rubbing against
her blindfolded face
and ejaculating
into her wounds.

Now
all she hears
is the numb rush
of water in her ears ...

fit to drown
in,
sink
in,
choke
in.

Die in.

Concetta closes the blinds,
trying to remember the sound
of the slats
slapping
shut
like the lens
of a digital camera.

With the artificial sunshine
blocked,
she lies down
and closes her eyes,
immersing herself
in a deeper darkness—a darkness
where the mere thought of song
evolves into a phantom
frequency rich
enough to imagine real.

She
stands
on a podium
in an embroidered silver gown,
her wild black curls
tamed
into a French twist,
face and lips

painted white,
eyebrows shaven
lashes plucked,
her diaphragm swelling
to the gentle vibration
... of peace.

A cappella.

Only the Queen
allows such luxury.
Only *He* may dress
his staff
in false expression;
allow a society
of assimilated skins
a sense of individualism,
and freedom
to express
emotion
through organic song.

She was headhunted by the assistants.

Concetta flicks
her eyes open
at the sound
of her own falsetto voice
hammering

through
her
head
like
a fire warning—she can
feel her glottis
open—blunt knife slicing
at the bottom of her vocal chords.

She must have only clicked *snooze*.

She listens
until the note softens
into a vibrato
like the flutter of butterfly wings,
clicking her tongue again
to switch it off.

*Just go
to the river.*

Concetta stands,
savouring
the sensation
of her silky lingerie
brushing
against her bony
thighs, buttocks
and shoulder blades,

as she slips it off.

She opens her wardrobe.

Beside her three
translucent
temperature-controlled bodysuits,
made from foetus membrane,
her old clothes hang
like limp, dismembered joints.

She pulls out a black lace corset,
with layers
of raw dark grey silk
and tulle
fanning out, into a skirt.

She remembers the day
she performed in it.

The curtain opened.
She tried not to squint
at the glaring white lights
or suck in the hanging silence
from the audience.

She had always feared
it might be contagious.
Someone in the audience gasped.

Another cried,
"I love you, Concetta!"
All rose, applauded
as if it were their cue;
a storm of flesh against flesh
clapping
the oxygen
from her lungs.

The power of their passion
climbed up her throat.
She wanted to smile.
But she couldn't.
Not permitted.
Mosè's orders:
"You'll never speak or smile.
You'll just sing.
That is your brand.
Mystery.
People will want to know more.
They will become curious.
You'll be the world's most famous opera singer
in no time.
You'll be an Idol.
Trust me."

She was.

Was.

Concetta closed her eyes.
Paper ruffled—a violinist's sheet music
perhaps, or Mosè adding up his pay check.

The orchestra waited for her first note.
She could sense their impatience,
Someone coughed, shushed.

She opened her eyes
to the lights turning
a dark red.

The sequins on her gown glowed
as if reflecting the bloodshot eyes
in the drugged crowd.

She took a deep breath;
her first notes hit
the stadium's walls—
a soprano earthquake: *Si comincia oggi ...*
A tender piccolo
trilled
before strings built
into a
Big
Brass
Boom.

The show received rave reviews.

They called her a cross
between Maria Callas
and Madonna.
"The only woman
to ever render
an audience of 100,000
mute in seconds,"
the reviewer wrote.

Perhaps I cursed myself that day.

Concetta tenderly lays
her dress on the bed,
fragile
and magical
as moth wings,
and closes the wardrobe door
on the bar-coded bodysuits.

Wear it.
What is there to lose?
I have nothing left
but lifeless skin and bone.

She stares at the dress
and touches
the rough fabric;
imagines a coarse sound
—corduroy on corduroy

as the tulle and silk collide
between her fingertips.

She clenches her jaw
and shuts her eyes,
envisions drowning
in the river

on the other side
of town,
wearing the dress.

She would step
into the water,
slowly
      moving
            down
                    the slipway
overgrown with   slick moss.

The skirt
of her dress
would float
around her thighs
like lily pads
before flicking up
around her taut nipples
like an inverted umbrella in wind.

The water
would soak
through the fabric,
staining it
with the decomposing fears of those
who have already succumbed

to the river's call,
and sink
with her
deaf | mute | corpse

Perfect.

***

The hum
of apprehension
invades Concetta's psyche
as she stands
in the dark, damp
lobby of her apartment building.

Graffiti plagues the walls
with voices of SOS calls

A black light reveals a letter
from her lover.
Written with the juices of his flesh.

Help
Yourself
—Yusuf.

Although she can't hear it,
she's sure the distant drip
of the cracked pipe
he cut himself with
still
echoes
against
the cold, concrete walls.

She used to sing
to that drip,
use it
as a metronome.

Drip
    Drip
        Drip ...

      .

      .

      .

    . *Si comincia oggi ...*

A trail of sound to Yusuf's flaming soul.
The Queen wears his skin.

She reaches for
the rusty door
handle, clutches
it, but does not
push it down.

She can feel her breath
quicken
to the beat
of self control
led astray; sweat
erasing in the lifelines
from her palms.

Saliva moistens
the walls of her mouth
and pools under her tongue.
She spits on the ground
to avoid the burn
in her mutilated throat.

It splashes before her bare feet.

At least they won't arrest me
for wearing shoes.

She opens the door
and steps outside.
The sunlight dimmed

to imitate
an overcast sky.
Grey. Matte—
a colour-blind toddler's
crayon scribble.

She saw
the radio-screen last night
forecast a chance of
controlled drizzle.

Passing heads turn
to greet her
with obligatory smiles,
but upon making eye contact
with her clothed body
they look at the ground
and scuttle away.

If a LEO,
pooned her,
the electric current
would travel outward
in a two meter radius from her.

She understands
innocent bystanders prefer
not to be caught in that.
The sensation—

your whole skeleton
being attacked
by streptococcus.
The searing sounds
permanently stamped to the brain,
designed to electro-jolt
you, thereafter,
with every fleeting flashback.

Concetta strides
down the street
toward the suburb's *reeleaver*,
one of twenty speed inducers
in the city,
praying
that once she obtains
a temporary speed implant,
she might make it
to the river
without being spotted
by a LEO.

Before she gets there
a busker playing
the harp, distracts her.
She pushes through
the naked crowd,
surrounding him.

Many are slathered with
poon-retardant gel—
a 200 ml gift
from the Queen
for being offense-free
in a succession of twelve months.

The non-gelled people
mutter and scurry
away, like ants
escaping a drop of rain.

The harpist stares
at Concetta;
his arms
moving up and down
like an ink scale on a treble clef.
His irises are such a pale brown
they look almost gold.

*Is he wearing contact
lenses? Are they legal?*

He doesn't seem fazed
by Concetta's clothed existence,
or the scar disfiguring her throat,
and tips his black-brimmed hat
in greeting,
clearly experimenting

with law-breaking
one tiny step
at a time.

She watches him,
leaning her weight on one foot,
and bites the nail
off her pinkie finger.
The crowd of bodysuits
glare
at the ground—
afraid of being accused
of condoning her presence.

More back away
like wriggling maggots,
as Concetta steps closer to him.

The harpist smiles
baring crooked, stained
teeth that match
the colour of his eyes.

Concetta stands at his side.
Her attempt at a smile
mimics an involuntary twitch.

He stops playing,
pushes the harp

forward
and gestures for her to sit
in his lap.

She obliges.
The harpist runs
his hands up her legs,
inching her dress
higher up her thighs.

With a sharp gasp, she grabs
his hands
with clawed fingers
to stunt their movement,
but he doesn't flinch.

Instead he spreads
her knees,
nestles the harp
between
them,
and rests the head
of the instrument
on her right shoulder.

He breathes into her neck.
The scent
of cinnamon
hovers

above her top lip.
She shivers,
inhaling its spicy sweetness.

The harpist reaches through
Concetta's arms
and around her waist
to pluck the strings.
His wrists move
with the grace
of a macrobiotic
symphony orchestra,
and the aroused pulse
between her legs.

Concetta places her hands over his,
so they barely touch the static
hairs on his knuckles,
shadowing his movement.

She closes her eyes
to feel the harmonic
ripples diffuse
through her limbs;
wishing these muted
underwater melodies
would turn her shadowy
royal blues
to gentle pastel corals

—to chords
of hope.

The harpist stops playing.
His desperate call
vibrates against Concetta's neck,
the heat of his words.

He pushes the harp
out of their way
and lifts Concetta to her feet
from under her arms.

She flicks open her eyes.
Standing before them
is a LEO, identifiable
by his gold-plated toenails.

He aims a gun,
not an *electropoon*,
at Concetta
with a trembling hand.

Not shock.
Death.

The harpist
raises his hands.
She raises hers too,

contemplating an escape.
She can make it to the river
without the speed implant.
She knows she can.
But outrun a bullet?

She will not be killed
and skinned
for their new-range
of temperature wear.
The LEO lowers his gun
and stares at the ground.
He shakes his head,
his shoulders move
up
and
down.

He sniffs
and lifts
his head
to look into the sky,
tears cascade
down his cheeks.
He mouths,
"What's the fucking point?"
and pokes the gun
underneath his chin.

Pulls the trigger.

The harpist jumps
backward, his chest
heaving, breath concertinaed.
The LEO's blood trickles
toward them.
Remaining bystanders flee.

He lowers himself
onto the stool,
staring at the dead
LEO.

Not a single blink.

He looks at Concetta,
removes his hat
with a crooked smile
and places it on the ground
upside-down.

Concetta takes off her dress.

She sits in the harpist's lap,
pulls the instrument
between her legs,
the harpist's hands
around her waist,

and places his fingers
on the strings.

He begins to play.

His warm Adam's apple moves
against her shoulder.

Concetta clutches
the harp's wooden frame
with both hands.
The vibrations
migrate up
through her arms,
her neck,
until she's certain
she can hear
the notes
pulse | into | her | temples

She will learn
how to play
the harp.

And sing in her sleep.

Si comincia oggi …

the end

she

AUTHOR'S NOTE

This story explores the notion that it's blasphemous for religion to be institutionalized, because no matter what one believes, there will always be something or someone that contaminates its worth. However, the content of this story is not in any way a direct criticism of religion, or a representation of my beliefs. It's simply a creative exploration of the concept.

I am nailed to white time.
Surrounded by space
and shallow breath.
All the thoughts I'd hoped
to forget, they swirl around
my head—the seeds
of non-existence;
condensation of infinity.

She turns them to cotton.
They crawl all over me,
tickle and sting like insects
disinfecting the lesions
that suck my heart dry
all day, all night—all life.

My body stiffens—cotton
memories draw sadness
through my dilating pores
to the surface of my skin.
Escape artists liquefied,
Each as unique as microscopic
tears. They gather and roll
and drip from the tips
of my fingers, flooding
the labyrinth that are my prints
with reflections of Father
using his to explore
how I feel inside.

I hover—waiting
for *She* to speak.

Don't be afraid, for I am with you.
Don't be discouraged, for I am your She, she, she ...

She's voice is a whisper, a shy child
I eagerly await her soft
white time, where time stands
still; where *She* cuts me,
breaks me, soothes me,
heals me, until I bleed silver
from where Father explored
with his labyrinths.
I see it happen, in the reflection
of my floating tears, before it does.
But I feel ...
how I have always wanted to feel.
Safe.
Lost.
In a place like heaven.
But not heaven at all.

I am not slow to fulfil my promise,
as some count slowness,
I am patient toward you,
not wishing that you should perish,
but that you should reach repentance.

I stand still—arms out
to the side, head hanging
like Jesus. Unable to move.
It seems like days.
The *whoosh* of silver tears
through my hands and feet
do not cause pain,
but heal my self-inflicted wounds.

If *She* lets me go
I would not want to.
I do not want to return home.
I like it here—wet with the sweat
of the past, no longer trapped
where it eats like acid to a corpse
from the inside out.

That's where it always started—
from inside—and ended
on the outside, in the form
of stigmata and release.
My mother would push
up my sleeves
and she would wet her face
with her own past
and hug me until
I feigned a seizure.

I never cry.

I puncture.

Now, for the first time in my life
I'm able to relish the throb
of pain in my heart, in my head,
and the ensuing relief,
as the weight in my chest,
in my limbs, liquefies
and dissolves
—like that moment at first light
when you open your eyes
and have forgotten the knot
in the back of your throat
from the memory
of Father's labyrinths;
exploring the years of self-hate,
where silver now pours from me
and deems me forbidden.

My body grows lighter
and quiet and small,
I lose traction
from the surface of time.
If there is a surface at all.

I look down.
At my feet.
they're bleeding too,
and so are my palms.

I'm completely naked,
anatomy omitted,
my breasts completely flat.
The shape of my body
androgynous.

I am inviolable.
A dove
in a glass box
thriving without air.

She, she, she ...

The sheen of white time
and space surrounding me
weakens in density
and the world spins, spins, spins ...
Around and about my head.
Around and fast and fleeting,
and closer and quicker and beating.
A tornado of air
gathers in my stomach
and I want to throw up.
I want the spinning to stop.

Make it stop! I scream.
Make it stop, stop, stop ...

It does.

There is silence.
And Aureole.

I lost her
when I was ten—I never saw
her again. It was all my fault.
I hadn't noticed
the unravelling
cord, the fibres splitting
like a burnt offering.
The leash snapped in the woods
schwack like the sound
of flagellation.

That day
the heavy-headed mornings
began to shadow the truth
with branches from
rotting sacred trees.

I was to blame.
I've hated myself ever since.
It's why Father tried
to cure me, move me, mould me;
scold me—make me plead
guilty, guilty, guilty ...

How could I have been so careless,
to neglect unconditional love?

Aureole licks blood
from my feet. My blood turns
silver on her tongue,
and the white time
and space returns; encases us
with the weightlessness
of freedom.
Acceptance.

I am nothing but zeros,
tumbling through tunnels,
tumbling through white holes,
in the universe.

And there appeared a great wonder in heaven;
a woman clothed with the sun,
and the moon under her feet, feet, feet …

Aureole whimpers
and walks backwards.
Her eyes widen as a knife
slices vertically down
the centre of my back.
As I open my mouth to scream,
the pain is soothed—a cold heat
flushes through my spine,
like stealing warmth
in a slither of sun in the snow.

Birds in flight flutter behind me.
Echo in slow motion;
fill the air with thick sound waves
make the encompassing white
sheen tremble
like quaking earth beneath the sea.

Feathers brush against the back
of my neck and whisper:
I am the resurrection and the life.
Whoever believes in me, though She die,
yet shall She live, and everyone who lives
and believes in me shall never die.
Do you believe this?

I turn my head.
They're not birds at all.
The sound is coming from ...

my wings, wings, wings ...

My arms tingle.
I hold my hands in front of me.
They're invisible,
but I can still make them
out—framed in silver light.
I rub my fingers together
and the light rubs off like ash.
And when I blow on the ash,

it sparkles in the air
like sun shining through mist.

I feel alive, for the first time
in my life. No heavy head,
no fears. No hiding.

No secrets.

Aureole sits,
and holds out her paw.
I smile, kneel beside her,
scratch below her chin.
I can sense my movements,
though I cannot see them,
my brain is reflecting
my thoughts into space—
holograms of intent.

We belong here.
Aureole and me.
Please, *She*, don't make us leave.

In the path of righteousness is life,
and in its pathway there is no death.
Do not withhold good
from those to whom it is due,
when it is in your power to do it.

She hums and strokes my wings,
rips them from my back.
But there is no pain—
just an all-encompassing emptiness.

She who conceals her transgressions will not prosper,
but she who confesses and forsakes them
will obtain mercy, mercy, mercy ...

She's voice
vibrates through my body,
kick-starting my pulse.

No, no, no!

I awake with a jolt,
a winded chest,
and a tube down my throat
that tastes like flesh.
I am lying down,
arms out to the side,
legs flattened to the white
bed—strapped down tight.
Lights flash in my eyes
as they are pried open
with stiff cold fingers.

A man murmurs:
She is lucky to be alive.

Monitors beep.
Mother soothes,
baby, please stop doing this,
She wipes my forehead
with a wet cloth
then gently kisses my hand.

My limbs ache.
My head aches.
My heart beats in my ears ...

... and I remember all the blood.

The release
staining the water
as I punctured my wrists with nails.
I drove them into my skin
with so much rage
I forgot I was hurting myself.
and not Father.

I close my eyes and swallow.
She's voice echoes in my head:
Do not withhold good
from those to whom it is due,
when it is in your power to do it.
And I picture the stray dog,
I feed every morning
at 9 a.m. sharp by our letter box.

Unconditional love.

I stare at the ceiling
as Mother rests
her head beside mine
and cries on my pillow.
The heavy drop
of each tear on starched linen
a mark of Mother's faith:

Guilt for Sundays.
        Pride for obedience.
                Guilt for silence.
                        Pride for sustained worship.

Father will be here soon, Mother says.
For you to repent.

Mother squeezes my arm with a sniff
as if acknowledging my pain—my fate—
is enough
for me forgive her.

I take a deep breath,
hold it until my vision blurs,
and my chest aches
as if being held down
by Father's weight.

I turn my head, and look
Mother in the eyes.
I see a reflection of *She*
her voice washes through me,
cleansing my veins
with absolution:

Don't be afraid, for I am with you.

But I am afraid.
I will always be afraid.

Of Father.
My Daddy.

My only road to *She*.

the end

acknowledgements

A massive thanks to my parents—Erika Bach and Demetri Vlass, Spilios—my one and only for life. And of course, a very special thanks to Amie McCracken for her enormous help in producing *The Bell Collection* edition.

The original version of *she* was first published in the anthology *Heroes of Phenomena: audiomachine*, edited by Samantha Redstreake Geary, under the title *Nailed to White Time*. The original version does not have a focus on religion, but on unconditional love and self-worth, and is suitable for young readers.

Heroes of PHENOMENA is a global, cross-industry collaborative campaign encouraging the next generation of authors, artists, and musicians. Epic motion picture advertising music production house, audiomachine, will make a donation to the Los Angeles Youth Orchestra with every download of the book.

A dedicated youth section showcases talented aspiring artists and authors from Elevate's Life & Art Studios, alongside inspiring industry professionals and the winning entries of PHENOMENA's Epic Heroes Event.

Other featured authors include: Darynda Jones, Amy Michele, Susan Kaye Quinn, M. Pax, Alex J. Cavanaugh, Crystal Collier, C. Lee McKenzie, and Ruth Long.

To read more about the project, please visit: *writerlysam.com/2014/06/07/heroes-of-phenomena-book-launch/*

Enjoyed this book?
Go to *vineleavespress.com/books*
to find more from *The Bell Collection*.

To sign up to Jessica's newsletter and/or connect with her on social media go to *jessicabellauthor.com/contact*.

Are you a writer?
You might be interested in Jessica's
Writing in a Nutshell series.

www.ingramcontent.com/pod-product-compliance
Lightning Source LLC
Chambersburg PA
CBHW030155070426
42447CB00032B/1203